BUILDING A BOAT

ALLEN BELCHER

WestBow Press books may be ordered through booksellers or by contacting:

WestBow Press
A Division of Thomas Nelson & Zondervan
1663 Liberty Drive
Bloomington, IN 47403
www.westbowpress.com
844-714-3454

ISBN: 979-8-3850-3276-1 (sc)
ISBN: 979-8-3850-3277-8 (e)

Library of Congress Control Number: 2024918084

Print information available on the last page.

WestBow Press rev. date: 10/20/2024

WESTBOW
PRESS®
A DIVISION OF THOMAS NELSON
& ZONDERVAN

I the Lord have made you the vessel of my purpose, I have taken you by the hand, and kept you safe, and I have given you to be an agreement to the people, and a light to the nations.

—Isaiah 42:6 (NIV)

Preface

My hope is that through reading the stories in this book, you see God in all His glory. It is only because of who He is and what He has done that this is even possible. I am just one example of how He leaves the ninety-nine to come for the one.

Suppose one of you has a hundred sheep and loses one of them. Doesn't he leave the ninety-nine in the open country and go after the lost sheep until he finds it? And when he finds it, he joyfully puts it on his shoulders and goes home. Then he calls his friends and neighbors together and says, "Rejoice with me; I have found my lost sheep" I tell you that in the same way there will be more rejoicing in heaven over one sinner who repents than over ninety-nine righteous persons who do not need to repent. (Luke 15:4–7 NIV)

Lastly, I want you to know that even though I do not know your face or your name, I have prayed for you.

Chapter 1

Emptiness Creates Opportunity (Hull)

Some people come to the realization that the emptying out of their lives is essential for their true purpose to be discovered through Christ at an early age. Others like myself struggle with this for many years of their lives before they surrender to God. The thought of going all in and giving up control was terrifying. Thoughts about what that would look like consumed my mind. Even feeling the pull toward God earlier in my life, I chose to run even harder away from God. I chased after the world and all it had for me. I found myself always chasing happiness, never ever knowing that there was something called joy out there. I was searching for what would give me temporary happiness because that is all this world can offer. It took me down many wrong turns in my life. I have broken every one of God's commandments. At one point in my life, I had a ten-year stint where I fought God daily. I hurt so many people in my life because of the hurt and hate that I carried around in myself. Later in the book, we will break down some of these situations and circumstances that I am referencing.

The main point that I do not want you to miss is that through all of this, I found myself empty. Through every broken dream, through every heartache, through every failure, and through all my success, I was still empty. At fifty years old, successful by world standards, I was hurt, broken, and empty. I came to the realization that money could not fix it, toys could not fix it, assets could not fix it, and even going to church couldn't fix it. That is when God started working on me and in me. I had tried religion for so many years, going in and out of churches. What I had never tried was a real relationship with Jesus. Now, I had been saved as a teenager in a church, but for the wrong reason. I was running from something, not toward someone. I got saved because I did not want to go to hell. No change happened, no turning point, no real experience. So, at fifty, I went all in with God, coming to Christ because I wanted to be in right relationship and because I wanted Jesus to be so many more names to me other than … Now I can say Jesus has been my Savior, my Protector, my Provider, my Healer, my Guidance, my Father, and best of all, my Friend. My life has changed, and God has blessed me in so many ways with my walk with Him. To God be all the glory and honor.

However, I will never forget the brokenness and emptiness that started this transformation. I will never forget trying to negotiate with God on how our relationship would be. I remember saying to a group of men that next weekend, I was going to stop cussing. I was saying this to the group to get someone to give me a pat on the back for trying this next step. What I received from my friend Tim was a slap on the face when he asked me, "What about today? Why not just do it today?" The timing was perfect. Let us face it; God's timing always is. The Holy Spirit was speaking through Tim and calling me out. It was what I needed at that time in my life. I needed to know that I had surrounded myself with a group of men who were going to challenge me. Men who would call me out when needed. This ten-second question changed my mindset. God used an obedient man to speak directly into me. I hope and pray that this book does just that in your life. I hope it allows your eyes to be opened and your vision to be restored so you may see God's wonderful plan for your life.

Gods plan is so perfect for our lives. What the devil thought was the end for Jesus when He breathed His last breath was just the promise of the beginning. Jesus rose from the grave and left it empty on the third day. The way the empty tomb was left is so significant. The linen was folded, which is in fact a promise that He is coming back. The tomb had to be made empty so the Holy Spirit could come and fill our emptiness.

Peter, however, got up and ran to the tomb. Bending over, he saw the strips of linen lying by themselves, and he went away, wondering to himself what had happened. (Luke 24:12 NIV)

If we can empty out our selfish desires, then God can fill us with what we need as we need it to complete His purpose for our lives. So never think of the words "surrender to God" as giving up. All we are doing is coming under the authority of Christ. We are just saying, "Here I am. Use me, Lord." We are not giving up; we are in fact getting fitted with the armor of God to go into battle.

The empty tomb is just the beginning. It is just where it all starts.

"Don't be alarmed," he said. "You are looking for Jesus the Nazarene, who was crucified. He has risen! He is not here. See the place where they laid him." (Mark 16:6 NIV)

Just like building this boat, it all starts with an empty hull. The emptiness of the hull means it is open and able to have what it needs added to make it ready to fulfill its purpose. The hull is reinforced multiple times with fiberglass and resin. This makes the hull stronger without compromising the openness. We are no different. We must be emptied out to be able to get what we need to fulfill our purpose in Christ Jesus. We have layers in us that are life experiences that have made us stronger and harder. However, the situations do not change our emptiness or our openness.

The hull is the foundation of the boat. It is what everything will be built on.

For no one can lay any foundation other than the one already laid, which is Jesus Christ. (1 Corinthians 3:11 (NIV)

The empty feeling that I spoke about earlier is how God found me. I did not perfect anything before coming to Christ. It is through Christ that we are made whole. It is all that Christ already did and nothing that I did or could do that made the difference.

The hull is not ready to go to water and be used for fishing yet. Just like our walk with the Lord, we have more that must be done in us before we can be used for discipleship. The starting point for us is getting our lives right with God.

If you declare with your mouth, "Jesus is Lord," and believe in your heart that God raised him from the dead, you will be saved. (Romans 10:9 NIV)

If you have never really given your life to God, do that now. It will be the best decision you will ever make in your life. It will also be the way to start this book with that empty hull that is needed for God to do a great work through you. This is an easy and painless process. All you need to do is pray this prayer to God:

Dear Lord Jesus, I know that I am a sinner, and I ask for Your forgiveness. I believe You died for my sins and rose from the dead. I turn from my sins and invite You to come into my heart and life. I want to trust and follow You as my Lord and Savior. God, thank You for filling me and for the guidance that You bring into my life. Amen.

Follow me as my disciples accepting me as master and I will make you FISHERS OF MEN

Matthew 4:19

Questions

1. What is keeping you from going all in with God?
2. How is you being in control and not allowing God to be the ruler in your life working out for you?
3. Stop doing what you have always done and expecting a different result. Give God a chance to lead your life and find your purpose. Why not today? Why not right now?

Chapter 2

The Support System (Stringers)

So many people, including myself, have tried to do it right at times in their lives, but it never seems to work out as we think it should. I think I have found what will help everyone understand some answers to the whys in their lives. Once I became saved and in a right relationship with God, I had a better understanding of God, and this has helped me find answers to some of the whys and why nots in my life. So many times in my life, I tried to do what I thought was right for me, my family, and even my job. I have learned that God answers prayers in three main categories: no, slow, and go.

When we pray about something, we want to hear God say yes. This is when we feel warm and fuzzy and love how good our God is. This is when we get to watch as God heals someone, saves a marriage, or helps with a financial situation, and the list goes on and on. These are the moments that we love to see from our prayers.

However, God also says to us that the timing is not right. These are the times when we push to see something done. Now, we may have great intentions, but it is just the wrong time. God's plan and timing are always perfect. These are the times when our understanding is stretched. This is when we pray earnestly and repeatedly. This is when we feel like maybe God is not hearing us. In reality, all God is doing is allowing all the details to come together as He wants for us. Remember God wants the best for us.

The last way God answers our prayers is by saying no. This is the one we do not like to talk about. We do not like to accept this one. We sure do not want to run around and tell everyone about it. However, the noes in my life have usually kept me from more pain.

An example of a no in my life that God blessed me with is my first day coming to Church of the Highlands. My family felt betrayed and like we had been stabbed in the back by a few people in a previous church. So many times, people think that the church had hurt them. In reality, it was people who caused the hurt. It is not the church that hurts people. The devil loves to try to convince people that the church is who hurts us. If this resonates with you, please know that the devil has fed you a lie. This was one of the hurts that I carried with me for many years, and I allowed it to fester in my life. It is true that hurt people hurt people. I hurt so many because of the inner pain that I was carrying around with me.

After years of not going to church, my daughter, who was fourteen at the time, asked me to try this new church that some of her friends were talking about. I agreed, and that Sunday, I held her hand on one side of me and my wife's hand on the other and headed toward the door. You know our God has a sense of humor and loves humility. The man holding the door that morning was one of the men who was at the center of our hurt from years ago at that previous church. My daughter had no idea and was swinging my hand with excitement. My wife was squeezing my other hand and rubbing my arm; she knew what thoughts and emotions were running through my mind. I was in spiritual warfare with about a hundred feet between me and a man who I felt had wronged me. To be blunt, I had hate in my heart that I had carried for years toward this man. I was fighting with God every step of those last one hundred feet. I was saying, "I cannot."

God was saying, "No, you cannot, but I can."

I had thoughts of kicking his shin as I walked by him. About twenty feet away, I remembered saying to God that I was leaving, and I remember God speaking to me for the first time in years. He said no and told me that I was going to be a man of my word and take my daughter to church because I'd told her I would. Again, a slap in the face—much needed and right on time, perfect. I will tell you that I did not speak as I walked the man by because I was thinking about something that my momma had told me. "If you don't have anything good to say, then don't say anything at all." I made my momma happy that day; I kept my mouth shut. I remember getting to our seats and leaning over to say to my wife that I was pretty sure this is not our church. When church started, it was great. The Holy Spirit could be felt from the first song, through the message, and even walking out of the building. I remember leaning over to my wife again as we walked out of the building to say that this just might be our church.

If I had not listened to God saying no to me, I may not have ever walked into that building. This one act of obedience has blessed me so much. Walking through that door that morning was a sign of obedience and humility for me personally. The group of men that I spoke of earlier were in a small group, and the Freedom conference is where I went all in with God. So the answer no in our prayer life can be one of the most impactful answers that we get.

I walked you through these responses to help you realize that not everywhere you may want support (stringer) in your vessel is necessarily where you *need* support. The cross braces that you see in the next picture are called stringers. They support not only the exterior hull against the waves and storms but they also support the weight of the boat and its contents.

A computer program takes the dimensions of the hull and then cuts the pattern for the stringers. The computer can compute how far apart the stringers can be and still support the boat. The computer considers how much stress the boat can take before the hull is compromised. It has a program that considers how much weight each area will need to support. The stringers are made from a waterproof composite material. Then the stringers are strengthened with multiple layers of fiberglass and resin to make sure they are strong and completely sealed. Another way to sum up what a stringer does is to say that it does all the strengthening and supporting of the boat. Then the stringers are filled with closed-cell foam to give a completely waterproof system of support and strength for the boat.

Now just like this boat must have support from two directions, we as men do too. My support system of my friends Mike and Shannon is one of my greatest blessings. To have two men and their families as my mentors and my encouragement at times and then allow me to pour back into them is absolutely amazing. These relationships only take a back seat to my relationships with my wife, children, and most importantly, God. It is vital to have Godly men in your life who pour into you as you pour into them.

As iron sharpens iron, so one man sharpens another. (Proverbs 27:17 NIV)

The second support we have is the strength from God the Father. The ability to know that He has got us is so great. A friend, David White, once told me that we have a job to do and God has a job to do; let us just not get in His way. Look at all the support that God gives. He does all the heavy lifting. God just wants our willingness and our obedience. Let Christ be the stringers in our lives. Just like a computer figured out where the stringers needed to be in the boat hull, God, who is our Creator, knows where our support needs to be. He already knows every hair on your head, so what makes you think He does not know us better than we know ourselves? Let God put your supports in place where they are needed so you can withstand the storms when they come and withstand the weight that you will need to carry at times in your life. Just look at some of the scriptures in God's Word when it comes to where our strength comes from.

I can do all this through him who gives me strength. (Philippians 4:13 NIV)

The Lord is my rock, my fortress and my deliverer; my God is my rock, in whom I take refuge, my shield and the horn of my salvation, my stronghold.

(Psalm 18:2)

Be on your guard; stand firm in the faith; be courageous; be strong.

(1 Corinthians 16:13)

I've yet to meet someone who went all in with God and has regrets. The strength that God gives us when we need it most is unimaginable. When a man put his hands on my daughter's throat when she was sixteen and tried to take her with him was when God gave me some of this strength.

I had peace throughout the entire process. From finding out the name of the man to having a conversation with him on the phone, God was with me. Never once lost focus on God and what He was doing; this was key. God gave me so much insight during this situation. First, He loves that man just like He loves me. Second, God was with my daughter the entire time. You may be wondering how I know that. Because the could haves and what ifs never happened. It was because He was there that the ending was good. God answered one of my prayers that night as He protected my family—finally giving me the ability to forgive the man through a phone call, and I mean really forgive him. The old me would have probably gone to prison, but God strengthens us when we are weak. It is that complete surrender that you read about prior. We all dreamed of being a super hero when we were kids. The reality as an adult is that there *is* such a thing as superhuman strength. It is God's strength. You should try it!

Questions

1. When has God answered one of your prayers with a clear no? Looking back, why was God's negative answer actually good for you?
2. Who is your support system in your life? What do they mean to you?
3. Where do you feel like you need extra support in your life?

Chapter 3

A Way Out (Hole in the Stringers)

God is a Waymaker. He makes a way when there seems to be no way. This is so true in our lives. I think about how many times in my life that God made a way. Remember this is the same man who ran from and fought God for ten years. I found myself headed down the wrong road during those years of my life, making decisions for temporary satisfaction, and trying to just get through this life the best way I knew how. These choices carried me so far down the wrong path that I did not even think God was near me anymore. The choices I was making with how I spoke to and raised my children were awful. The way I mistreated my wife and how I allowed my kids to see and hear that was nothing short of abusive. It did not just happen in the four walls that I called home, but it bled over into my work life and other relationships.

There was one night where I decided to do something that could possibly change my life forever. At 10:32 that night, the Holy Spirit spoke to me. He had not spoken to me in years, but He did this night. It was plain and clear. He said, "Don't do this; not this. You will never recover." I was at a dead-end road with nothing but death and destruction staring back at me. God showed up for me that night and provided that hole I needed to get the evil out. It was just a simple pathway. But for me, in that moment, it was probably what allowed me to be a free man today. It was years later that I found my verse about what that 10:32 moment meant to me.

Whoever acknowledges me before others, I will also acknowledge before my Father in heaven. (Matthew 10:32 NIV)

God made a path for me that night. However, His words to me that night also carried a choice. It was my call to action. Thank you, Lord God, for guiding me and making a path for me that night.

Show me your ways, Lord, teach me your paths. (Psalm 25:4 NIV)

I walked in the day after they had finished wrapping and strengthening the stringers. It had taken a few days to get the stringers right. Remember that 100 percent waterproof and sealed was what they had told me that they'd been working toward.

I rounded the corner and there was a guy who I had not met yet in the boat. He was drilling holes in the bottom of the waterproof stringers, where water is the enemy. I was trying to talk to him, but this man did not speak English. I panicked. I hurried to find the owner because this guy was making a hole in what we had worked on for days. In my mind, he was making a mistake.

Once I found the owner, he said, "No matter how good of a material we use, and no matter how good of a job we do putting it together, the water is still going to get in." He reassured me that the holes were correct and needed to let the water (enemy) get out when it did find a way in. The man's name who was drilling the holes in the boat was Jesus.

No matter how good a job you do with your quiet time, Bible reading, prayer life, and walk with Jesus, evil is still going to get into your life at some point. It is the same way with a boat. No matter how much waterproof material is used in and on the stringers, the water will still penetrate. So the purpose of the freshly drilled hole in the stringer is to allow a way for the water to get out. The hole is no more than a pathway in the stringer. Our lives are the same; Jesus made a way for us through the holes in His hands, His feet, and His side.

Trust in the Lord with all your heart and lean not on your own understanding;

in all your ways submit to him, and he will make your paths straight.

(Proverbs 3:5–6 NIV)

Sometimes in life, I think we get blinded to what God can do because we focus so much on what we cannot do. If I focused on my past and my sins and shortcomings, I would walk around defeated, because I messed it up. I made a mess of everything for so long that it just became what I expected. Lying, stealing, deceiving, cheating, manipulating, and so on are just the beginning of who I was.

Then God showed up. When God took control of my life, things just started working out. My wife is the person in my life who showed me what the saying "love like Jesus does" means. She kept me when she could have left me. She never nagged at me but, instead, talked to God about me. For thirty years, she prayed for my path. She prayed for a breakthrough, a hole in what seemed to be a strong and impenetrable wall. When God answered her prayers and I went all in, things changed drastically. Getting the spiritual order right for the first time in our home was huge for our family.

We have watched as our children have developed a deeper relationship with God than ever before in their lives. The honor that I get to give to God for all He has done is indescribable. Hearing my son say to our small group that he just had to come see what changed his dad because the man before him now is not the man he grew up with wrecked me. On one hand, I was so thankful for all that God has done with me. On the other hand, I am so sorry for the life I once lived. Through that statement, God began to work on me deeper. I am not proud of anything that I did when I was not living for God. However, God wants to use all that hurt, pain, and disappointment to help others.

You intended to harm me, but God intended it for good to accomplish what is now being done, the saving of many lives. (Genesis 50:20 NIV)

Getting to the point where I could forgive myself for my past was one of the best moments of my life. God is so good and so faithful. Look for your path that He is providing you.

Questions

1. What evil gets through all your precautions to creep into your life?
2. What would you say was your 10:32 moment in your life where you knew God was speaking to you?
3. What do you need to help remove the evil from your life?

Chapter 4

Our Connection and Source
(Fuel Tank and Wiring)

The relationship with the Holy Spirit is so vital to our walk with God. God the Father, the Son, and the Holy Spirit. Feeding our spirit is key to a healthy walk with God. If we feed our mind or our soul more than we feed our spirit, our spirit gets silent, like when you read previously about my 10:32 moment. That happened because I was feeding everything but my spirit. To feed our spirit we need to use our quiet time, prayer life, Bible reading, and worship songs and we need to listen to messages.

Jesus answered, "It is written: 'Man shall not live on bread alone, but on every word that comes from the mouth of God." (Matthew 4:4 NIV)

These are all forms of feeding our spirit, but the key is your one-on-one time with God. Sometimes in life, we get caught up in all the noise of this world and think that when we go to God, we need to do all the talking. This is so far from the truth. We need time to listen for God's whisper also. I made the comment to my friends that I want to be so in tune with God's voice that I can hear when He takes a breath. That breath is when God is getting ready to speak.

He says, "Be still, and know that I am God. (Psalm 46:10 NIV)

We must set up constant communication with the Holy Spirit to be able to hear from God.

Your word is a lamp for my feet, a light on my path. (Psalm 119:105 NIV)

Being devoted to getting into the Word of God is how you will begin to hear God speak to you. God's Word will lead and guide you. It will speak to you through good and bad times in your life. My favorite reason for getting into God's Word is that God's Word is our only offensive weapon to fight spiritual warfare with.

Finally, be strong in the Lord and in his mighty power. Put on the full armor of God, so that you can take your stand against the devil's schemes. For our struggle is not against flesh and blood, but against the rulers, against the authorities, against the powers of this dark world and against the spiritual forces of evil in the heavenly realms. Therefore put on the full armor of God, so that when the day of evil comes, you may be able to stand your ground, and after you have done everything, to stand. Stand firm then, with the belt of truth buckled around your waist, with the breastplate of righteousness in place, and with your feet fitted with the readiness that comes from the gospel of peace. In addition to all this, take up the shield of faith, with which you can extinguish all the flaming arrows of the evil one. Take the helmet of salvation and the sword of the Spirit, which is the word of God.

And pray in the Spirit on all occasions with all kinds of prayers and requests. With this in mind, Be alert and always keep on praying for all the Lord's people. (Ephesians 6:10–18 NIV)

God has given you the ability to put the armor on daily. You must get dressed anyway, so why not put on the armor of God? You must make a choice; make the right one. The steps you take toward God through obedience will lead to such a closer relationship with Jesus. You are looking for the relationship to grow and get to the point where you hear God's voice. God still speaks to us today; He has just chosen not to use a burning bush to do so.

Now Moses was tending the flock of Jethrohis father-in-law, the priest of Midian, and he led the flock to the far side of the wilderness and came to Horeb, the mountain of God. There the angel of the Lord appeared to him in flames of fire from within a bush. Moses saw that though the bush was on fire it did not burn up. So Moses thought, "I will go over and see this strange sight—why the bush does not burn up." When the Lord saw that he had gone over to look, God called to him from within the bush, "Moses! Moses!"

And Moses said, "Here I am." (Exodus 3:1–4 NIV)

One key part of this scripture is that Moses had to move. He had to step toward the bush before God spoke to him. This is so key in our lives today. We must move toward God to hear from Him. We must put action with our words. Without this connection with God, we are lost. We wander around in life aimlessly and just get by. We try to do something in life that makes us feel good about who we are because we feel we *are* pretty good. However, do not fool yourself. You can never earn your way into heaven. It is a free gift to us that was paid for by the blood of our Savior and Lord Jesus Christ.

All these items in the next picture—the fuel tank, steering cables, and wire for the power source—are crucial for the boat to run and operate properly. Getting this connection right is the only real thing that matters. Without that "connection," the boat does not run and is instead tossed and moved by the winds and waves wherever they choose. Not only does God have the ability to make our boat run but he also has the ability to control the environment that the boat is in.

Then he got into the boat and his disciples followed him. Suddenly a furious storm came up on the lake, so that the waves swept over the boat. But Jesus was sleeping. The disciples went and woke him, saying, "Lord, save us! We are going to drown!"

He replied, "You of little faith, why are you so afraid?" Then he got up and rebuked the winds and the waves, and it was completely calm.
(Matthew 8:23–26 NIV)

Questions

1. How is your connection to the Holy Spirit?
2. How and what are you feeding your body? What do you need to cut out of your life because it is feeding the wrong source?
3. When is a time in your life that your boat was being tossed by the storms of life? Did you call on Jesus to calm the storms?

Chapter 5

What Covers Us (Capping the Hulls)

Multiple thoughts come to mind as I think about this next step in building the boat. The capping process is one that covers so much that has happened so far. You would not know the strength or material of the stringers if you did not see them before they were covered. All you would know is that the boat is gray and white. Looks good; feels good and strong. However, all the parts and sections that were just covered up are where the strength of the boat comes from. See, we had to complete the work in the bottom hull before we were ready to add the top hull.

Our life is just like that. Our life is like the bottom hull of this boat. It is the lesser part of the boat but does not function separately from the deck hull. However, to fulfill our purpose, we must be capped like the boat. When the deck hull is added, then the bottom can function as it was intended. Its purpose can be fulfilled. The deck is where the steering takes place. The deck is in complete control of what the hull does. It controls the boat, sets the direction, and controls from the top. The deck is responsible for the well-being of the bottom hull. The hull takes refuge under the deck. Before God comes into us, we are incomplete and without purpose because we've never had our guidance deck. Everywhere that we are insufficient, God is more than enough. Every time we are lost, He is there to light our paths. There is just so much more of God than we can understand.

My God is my rock, in whom I take refuge, my shield and the horn of my salvation. He is my stronghold, my refuge and my savior. (2 Samuel 22:3 NIV)

When I think of two becoming one, I cannot help but think of a wedding. After all, God's Word says that we are the bride of Christ. Men, what do we do when we find that special lady? Not just any lady, but *the* lady.

We take a knee. Without even thinking about it, we do two distinct things when we kneel. Firstly, we are letting her know that we've chosen her. We are making a public display of us choosing her. Secondly, we are submitting to her by presenting ourselves at her feet. We are saying that even though we've made our choice, we are now humbling ourselves at her feet and that it is her turn to be in control of what happens next. Men, we are looking for that special word—*yes*. It is no different with Christ. When choosing Jesus there is a public display like kneeling, but it is called baptism. We need to follow God's Word and allow people to see publicly that we choose Christ.

But whoever disowns me before others, I will disown before my Father in heaven. (Matthew 10:33 NIV)

Next, we must submit ourselves at His feet. If we lay ourselves at the feet of Jesus, He will take us places we've never dreamed of. Remember, as my friend says, that we have a job to do and God has a job to do and let us not get in the way. Think about that for a minute. If the Bible is true—and it is—and God's Word says He wants to prosper us—and He does—then why not submit to Him and fall under His authority? Stop trusting God with only your life after death. Step into all that God has for you and trust Him with every step every day. Trust Him with your life now. This is a part of the order that God has for each of us. Our God is a god of order. Spiritual order, to be exact. He is not a god of chaos. Let me show you something that I have found to be so good in my walk with God.

Submit yourselves, then, to God. Resist the devil, and he will flee from you. (James 4:7 NIV)

Look at the order of this verse. You are to submit yourselves first to God. Only at that point can you resist the devil, and he will therefore flee. If you get the order wrong, it will not work. You will be trying to resist the devil by yourself. The devil is not scared of you, and you will not make the devil flee. Only when you keep God first in the equation does the devil flee. Stop trying to do it alone. Use this next scripture as a prayer to God.

But you, Lord, are a shield around me, my glory, the One who lifts my head high. I call out to the Lord, and He answers me from His holy mountain. I lie down and sleep; I wake again, because the Lord sustains me. I will not fear though tens of thousands assail me on every side. (Psalm 3:3–6 NIV)

Questions

1. Who guides your boat through life? Are you trying to steer yourself, or have you asked Jesus to take the wheel?
2. Have you followed through with believer's baptism once you fully surrendered to God?
3. In what situation in your life did you mess up the order of putting God first?

Chapter 6

Finding Our Way (Navigation and Lights)

The screen in the picture shows us where waypoints are marked and where the fish holes are. The screen is what I keep my eyes and focus on while I am moving the boat from place to place. It has a chart app that shows me direction and provides me a straight path to stay on when getting to my destination. The plotter takes a destination that is not even on the screen and sets a straight path to it. The screen may only show me a line to the destination, but the plotter can see the destination even when I cannot.

In our lives, this would be akin to keeping our eyes focused on God and staying in His Word. God's vision is so much greater than our own. We know our destination—heaven. But just like the plotter, God sees the path and the destination along with everything on the path.

A voice of one calling in the wilderness, "Prepare the way for the Lord, make straight paths for him.

Every valley shall be filled in, every mountain and hill made low. The crooked roads shall become straight, the rough ways smooth.

And all people will see God's salvation." (Luke 3:4–6 NIV)

We lose focus and sometimes struggle to simply stay on the line that is headed to our destination. If we can just keep our eyes on Jesus, we will always be where we are needed at the time we need to be there. I have seen this first hand so many times in my life.

A great example of this is a fishing trip where our very first Fishers of Men group went fishing. The boat was made ten months before the trip. The vision for the group was discussed eight months prior to the trip. We had twelve men signed up to take the first group three months prior and booked a guide ten weeks prior to the day. Oh, and we changed the date of the trip ten weeks out as well.

While fishing on our trip that we had planned for months in advance, our guide, and my friend, Kelly received a phone call telling him that his family had been in a bad accident. Everyone was fine, but both cars were totaled. Perspectives changed. Life and living suddenly became the most important aspect of the trip. With tears in his eyes, Kelly talked about how good God is. Without even realizing it, he was giving his testimony to just how good God had been in his life. Thank You, Lord God, for being with his family and protecting them that day.

We caught trout and redfish that day, but the biggest "catch" was Kelly and what happened in his life. Remember my friend Shannon? He was on the boat with us. He was able to speak of life and love with Kelly. At that moment, Shannon was able to be salt and light. God's plans and timing are always perfect. The catch God had that day was already standing on the deck of the boat upon our arrival to go fishing that morning.

God, just like the screen, keeps my path straight. He guides me from one point in my walk to the next. God sees my future and has lined up every day that will come in my life in this world.

You have searched me, Lord, and you know me. You know when I sit and when I rise; you perceive my thoughts from afar. You discern my going out and my lying down; you are familiar with all my ways. Before a word is on my tongue you, Lord, know it completely. You hem me in behind and before, and you lay your hand upon me. Such knowledge is too wonderful for me, too lofty for me to attain. Where can I go from your Spirit? Where can I flee from your presence? If I go up to the heavens, you are there; if I make my bed in the depths, you are there. If I rise on the wings of the dawn, if I settle on the far side of the sea, even there your hand will guide me, your right hand will hold me fast. If I say, "Surely the darkness will hide me and the light become night around me," even the darkness will not be dark to you; the night will shine like the day, for darkness is as light to you. For you created my inmost being; you knit me together in my mother's womb.

I praise you because I am fearfully and wonderfully made; your works are wonderful, I know that full well. My frame was not hidden from you when I was made in the secret place, when I was woven together in the depths of the earth. Your eyes saw my unformed body; all the days ordained for me were written in your book before one of them came to be. How precious to me are your thoughts, God! How vast is the sum of them! Were I to count them, they would outnumber the grains of sand—when I awake, I am still with you. (Psalm 139:1–18 NIV)

The light Shannon was being to Kelly in that moment was like the lights on the boats that we use for navigation. The navigation lights on the boat are not for us to see how to navigate in the darkness but for others to be able to see where we are. It is for others to know there is a boat right there. We must be the light in a dark world. We must be able to be seen by others. Your light is part of who you are, what you do, and how you show you love of Jesus through it all.

Questions

1. Who guides your day-to-day decisions? What source are you depending on to guide you?
2. Do you trust God's line He has for you to follow, or are you still trying to set your own course?
3. Are you allowing your light to shine so others can see you? How are you displaying your light?

Chapter 7

The Finishing Touches (Accessories)

The accessories on the boat have such a meaningful purpose also. The radio is used for emergency communication. It is what I will use if there is ever a problem and I need to get help immediately.

Prayer is our way of communicating with God. Too many times in life, we use it as a form of emergency communication, like the radio. However, God intended prayer to be our everyday and anytime communication with Him. It was not designed to be a when-all-else-fails emergency call. God designed our communication channel (prayer) to be constant. We do not have to take a number or wait in line. Understanding the next verses will guide you through your prayers with God.

Ask and it will be given to you; seek and you will find; knock and the door will be opened to you. For everyone who asks receives; the one who seeks finds; and to the one who knocks, the door will be opened. (Matthew 7:7–8 NIV)

The leaning posts have room for eight fishing rods. There are several storage lockers, a cooler for keeping drinks cold, and a fish box to put our fish we catch. This boat was created for more than one person. It was made to hold multiple people.

In our lives, we are not made to be alone but to have friends in our lives whom we share time and activities with. We have places for their rods and reels, space for all the snacks, and multiple directions that our brothers in Christ can throw their bait out while standing shoulder to shoulder to catch fish. We always catch more fish if we have more fishermen. There is power in numbers.

For where two or three gather in my name, there am I with them.

(Matthew 18:20 NIV)

The motor is what powers the boat. The motor does not do anything until it is cranked and put into gear. I do all of this on the boat, but remember I am following the screen to get to where I am going. So I am really just going where my guidance system is telling me to go.

It is the same with my walk with Christ. I may be holding the wheel but I am going wherever He leads. It is called going all in. It is like sitting in a chair. You trust in and have faith that the chair will hold your weight. When you let God lead, by your faith, you are trusting God to hold you up. The first time you sit in the chair, you may sit slowly and be careful how you distribute your weight. But as you sit in the chair more and more, you will begin to know that it will support you. God is who created you. He knows you better than you even know yourself. You can trust Him.

In their heart's humans plan their course, but the Lord establishes their steps. (Proverbs 16:9 NIV)

Have I not commanded you? Be strong and courageous. Do not be afraid; do not be discouraged, for the Lord your God will be with you wherever you go. (Joshua 1:9 NIV)

The anchor is what holds the boat and keeps the current from taking it away to drift aimlessly. I cannot even tell you how many times Christ has been my anchor. When the world starts getting loud and it seems my world is crashing, I have peace knowing that my anchor in Jesus holds through it all.

An example of this is to not to put your faith, hope, and trust in humans. I love my wife, children, and my friends. But I promise, if I were their anchor, I would let them down. Not intentionally. It would just happen. I would forget to call them back, or I would forget to do something. I would just simply fall short of a perfect expectation. Thank the Lord that they do not consider me their anchor. Because I would slip and slid around, never really having that dependable hold. But with God, there is never a slip or slide. The anchor just holds tight. This world is a battleground, and too many of us are treating it like a playground. You must have an anchor that is strong and will hold through the storms. So make sure who your anchor is!

We have this hope as an anchor for the soul, firm and secure. (Hebrews 6:19 NIV)

Questions

1. How many times do you have only emergency communication with God? Explain.
2. Who are the people who are going to be on your boat with you? Why?
3. Do you feel like you have the right anchor in your life? How good does it hold when the storms come your way?

Chapter 8

The Name Matters (The Boat's Name)

Finally, I can add the name on the boat. The Holy Spirit was speaking to me prior to even beginning to build the boat. I knew what the name was going to be from the start. *Fisher of Men* was what the boat was to be called. I love the sticker that I placed on the dash that reads, "We catch them and He cleans them."

This reminds me so much of my friend David White, who I have referenced a couple of times already. He is one of my pastors at Church of the Highlands in Columbus, Georgia. He is the man who said, "We have a job to do, and God has a job to do; let's not get in His way." This man saw me walk into church on the first day with my hands in my pockets and not speaking to anyone. He said, "Good morning. Glad you are here." He loved me from the distance that I needed until one day we shook hands. Months later, we went to lunch so we could just get to know each other. During that conversation, I asked what he saw in me that first day. His response was that he saw a hardened man. This was so true. But just like the sticker on the dash, he was instrumental in catching me and then allowing God to clean me. This man was a big part in getting me to the point where God took over.

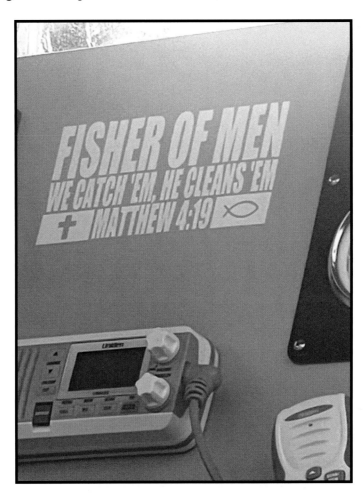

"Come, follow me," Jesus said, "and I will send you out to fish for people."

(Matthew 4:19 NIV)

Simon had been fishing all night and was tired, and I am sure he was frustrated. He had caught nothing all night long. He was just minding his own business and cleaning his nets when Jesus came to the shore. After getting on Simon's boat, Jesus finished preaching to the crowd. Once finished, Jesus told Simon to let down the net one more time. I think Simon did it not expecting a catch but just because he did not want to fight with or disrespect Jesus. The net was so full of fish that Simon had to call for another boat to come help get the catch loaded into the boats. I do not think it took Simon long to decide to follow Jesus.

That is the God we serve, gentlemen. He is the God of more. God has so much more in store for you than you can even comprehend. Do not misunderstand that previous statement. I do not serve God because of what He can do for me. I serve God because of what He has already done for me.

It is because of what He has already done that I know what He is capable of. God took me with all my brokenness and all my sins and showed me how much love He has for me. Telling my story to you is just a small part of the big picture. You telling your story is part of the picture as well. These last two statements are how we make a difference in the kingdom of God.

They triumphed over him by the blood of the Lamb and by the word of their testimony. (Revelation 12:11 NIV)

Once you are saved, the devil cannot have your soul anymore. So he tries to come after your testimony. He tries to instill fear, embarrassment, and doubt in your mind. Keep in mind that the devil is a liar. The Bible refers to him as the lord of lies. The truth is that your testimony will touch someone. What God did in your life will matter. You will find that just by telling your testimony, it will help others in their walk with Christ.

You are the salt of the earth. But if the salt loses its saltiness, how can it be made salty again? It is no longer good for anything, except to be thrown out and trampled underfoot. You are the light of the world. A town built on a hill cannot be hidden. Neither do people light a lamp and put it under a bowl. Instead, they put it on its stand, and it gives light to everyone in the house. In the same way, let your light shine before others, that they may see your good deeds and glorify your Father in heaven. (Matthew 5:13–16 NIV)

Just like I named the boat, God has named us. We are called the children of God. Sons and daughters of the Lord of lords and King of kings. God called us to be different, to stand out and separate ourselves from everything the world says is normal. The Bible uses words and phrases like *chosen*, *made in the image of God*, *head and not the tail*, *redeemed*, *saints*, and my favorite of all, *disciple* to describe us. This is how our God sees us.

Now if we are children, then we are heirs—heirs of God and co-heirs with Christ, if indeed we share in his sufferings in order that we may also share in his glory. (Romans 8:17 NIV)

Questions

1. What does your name mean biblically? What does that mean to you?
2. Name the people who have been a part of you becoming a Christian. Take a few minutes to let the ones you can know what that means to you.
3. What is your testimony? Tell others what God has done in your life and how He changed your life.

Chapter 9

Does It Float? (Maiden Voyage)

The day was finally here. It was time to take the boat to Florida to test it out. The term excited was a massive understatement for how I was feeling. Part of me was so happy to have a boat and then part of me was still asking God what this was all about. All I could do was smile and thank God. However, at that moment, His purpose was not completely revealed to me.

And we know that in all things God works for the good of those who love him, who have been called according to his purpose. (Romans 8:28 NIV)

So the three of us went out on the first trip. The engine had specific instructions on how it needed to be ran to break it in correctly. We had to run it at a certain RPM for a set time. This took several hours and was extremely frustrating because we all wanted to see what the boat could do. Finally, we completed the slow break-in phase and were ready to get the boat up on plane. We went across the bay into the ocean and went out to try some trolling. The seas were one to two feet, so it was not bad. The boat was doing great.

We decided to ease on out to one of our bottom numbers to see what we could get to happen. We had not been fishing long when a storm blew in from the land, and we knew we had to head back. So we fired the engine and started back toward land. About half way back to shore a bay boat came by us flying, and by now, the seas were four to five feet. The boat was coming completely out of the water as it hit wave after wave.

About a mile later, we came upon that boat, and something had broken on it. They were taking on water but still under power and moving pretty well. We pulled up about thirty feet away to talk to them. They were younger men and were in full panic mode. We were trying to just encourage and reassure them that it was going to be alright. The young man driving panicked, lost control of his thinking and actions, and ran straight into the side of my boat. His boat came over the side of my boat and was three feet into my boat directly in front of the center console area.

Some real stern calm downs were given, and we told them to turn and go straight at the beach. We immediately distanced ourselves from the other boat but remained in sight of them as we entered back into the bay. This trip would prove to be one of the greatest learning experiences for me in my walk with God.

In life, it happens just that quickly. We are just going about our day, our lives, our plans, and *wham*—divorce, job loss, sickness, or even death comes our way. That is how it went from one foot to four-foot seas and another boat hitting us. However bad it seemed, the boat performed its purpose. With all the storms and waves, it stayed floating. When the other boat hit us and ran on top of us, our boat stayed floating. As we rode back into the calm of the bay, it leveled up, smoothed out, and just continued to do what it was created to do. Our walk with God should be like the boat that day.

Being a Christian does not change the chaos of the world. It does not change the storms in our lives. It does not change the actions of other people that affect us. However, it does give us peace through the storm. It gives us hope and faith that we will make it. It is like putting on a raincoat and walking out in the rain. The coat does not make the rain stop. It just keeps us protected from the rain. The calm that I had during that situation was from the peace that the Holy Spirit was filling me with. It is the same peace that is available to each of us daily. See, just like this boat was made for something and has a purpose, so do we. You and I are just like the boat. We are made for something. We are set apart and given a unique set of gifts and skills from God that we are to use to fulfill His purpose in our lives. Do not confuse the words *His* and *our* in the previous sentence. This is how so many of us have lived life for too long.

Many are the plans in a person's heart, but it is the Lord's purpose that prevails. (Proverbs 19:21 NIV)

My plan that day was to test out the boat. Well, I guess we can check that box. We tested the boat in more ways than I could've imagined that day. God wants more for us than we can even comprehend. If you ever get to the point in your life where you say it is all about God, you will *not* regret that decision. The person staring back at you in the mirror is both the problem and the answer. Get out of the way! See, just like this first trip, I had a plan. I had a vision of what I thought and saw. However, God knew months earlier when we were building the stringers what would happen that day. God knew that it was important for me to know and see the strength of the boat and what it could handle. God knew I would need to know what I was standing on and in that day. So God prepared me when I was not even ready. He showed me what I needed to see to be ready for this day.

The Lord himself goes before you and will be with you; he will never leave you nor forsake you. Do not be afraid; do not be discouraged. (Deuteronomy 31:8 NIV)

I felt the presence of God with us that day, and His peace was so heavy that it was like raindrops from a storm. My prayer is that at some point in each of our lives, we get to experience what I felt that day. That peace that passes all understanding. While the seas were raging, and even when a boat hit us, God's peace was so profound.

The boat has one small scratch from the situation that day. My life, however, is full of many scratches from where the storms of this world have left me scarred. I am sure the boat will have more as well one day. These are reminders of the past; however, do not live in those moments. Keep your eyes on Jesus and what He is doing in your life today. It is the next trip you take that may be your best one yet.

Questions

1. How are you stepping into your purpose for God?
2. What kind of storms are you dealing with right now in your life? Are you trying to handle them, or are you allowing God to handle them?
3. If being in the middle of the storm was where you knew God would give you His peace, would you ask God for the storm?

Chapter 10

Can We Fish on Land? (Discipleship)

We do not need a boat to fish. In fact, we do not even need water to fish. One of my favorite parables in the Bible is where Jesus fed the five thousand. He did this with only two fish and five loaves of bread. It is one of my favorites because it shows the compassion Jesus had for the crowd who had gathered. It also showed how not only were there still so many people to teach but He also had so much more to teach the disciples.

The number twelve is used so many times in the Bible. Just my thought here, but I wonder if Jesus had specifically twelve baskets left so that each disciple would have to look at the leftovers right in their very hands?

When Jesus heard what had happened, he withdrew by boat privately to a solitary place. Hearing of this, the crowds followed him on foot from the towns. When Jesus landed and saw a large crowd, he had compassion on them and healed their sick. As evening approached, the disciples came to him and said, "This is a remote place, and it's already getting late. Send the crowds away, so they can go to the villages and buy themselves some food." Jesus replied, "They do not need to go away. You give them something to eat." "We have here only five loaves of bread and two fish," they answered. "Bring them here to me," he said. And he directed the people to sit down on the grass. Taking the five loaves and the two fish and looking up to heaven, he gave thanks and broke the loaves. Then he gave them to the disciples, and the disciples gave them to the people. They all ate and were satisfied, and the disciples picked up twelve basketfuls of broken pieces that were left over. The number of those who ate was about five thousand men, besides women and children. (Matthew 14:13–21 NIV)

So what is a disciple? A disciple is someone who follows Jesus, is changed by Jesus, and is committed to the mission of Jesus. God has called all of us to be disciples. Do not forget the key verse that inspired the boat's name.

Come, follow me," Jesus said, "and I will send you out to fish for people."

(Matthew 4:19 NIV)

Fishing for people is so rewarding. The blessings that flow from a catch are beyond explanation, but I am going to try. I think about two specific days that I think will help bring perspective. This day, and that day. If you knew *this* was the last day, what would you do? How would you spend your last twenty-four hours before going to heaven? I think most would answer to spend time with my family and friends, to make sure one is right with God, and maybe even talk to someone about God. Whatever your answer, it is the last thing you would be able to do.

However, we would all think about *that* day also. That day is the day after it all ends here. That day is where we get to see Jesus. We all want to leave a legacy. We all want to be remembered. Right? But here or there is the question. Are we looking for awards or rewards? The better way to ask it is are we focused more on this day or that day? So what we do here has to matter there. What we do this day needs to make a difference on that day. I believe that if you start to focus on just these two days, your life will change drastically. Just a few of the things that help me stay focused on these two days are my quiet time with the Lord, my prayer time, and my conversations and time with my two friends Mike and Shannon. Men, the last part of this is so vital to my well-being. Having the chance to speak into and to be spoken into by two men of God is so vital.

As iron sharpens iron, so one man sharpens another. (Proverbs 27:17 NIV)

Find yourselves godly men who you can do life with. Having men who can pour back into you as you pour out into others will be a key to longevity.

Questions

1. Who comes to your mind when you think of someone who needs help finding Jesus? What are you doing to help lead them?
2. If today was your last day, what would you do? Would you do anything this day for that day?
3. Who discipled you at some point in your life and helped you find Jesus? Who will say your name?

Chapter 11

Having the Right Tackle (Different Lures)

When my friends and I go fishing, the tackle we use changes depending on what we are targeting. If we are going after trout and redfish, we use medium rods with a Penn 3000-4000 reel. We put thirty-pound test braids on and use 1/0 hooks. Sometimes we even use a popping cork with artificial lures. But if we are going after snapper and grouper, we use a much heavier pole with a large offshore reel. We have eighty-pound braids on it and use a 6/0-8/0 hook. The difference in the tackle and lures matter.

Being a fisher of men is no different. We are trying to put the right message in front of the right people to watch as God moves in their lives. However, sometimes when we are out deep-sea fishing, we take a thirty-pound line rod and drop down a jerk bait. Catching a fish on light tackle is a challenge and a lot of fun. Sometimes a big fish will bite a smaller bait. Sometimes when you are targeting a smaller species of fish, you end up surprised with what you catch.

This happened a few weeks back with my friend Shannon. See, Shannon is part of the FCA and works with several schools where he devotes time speaking to the athletes in various sports. He takes time away from his job, his lunch hour, and even time from his family on occasion to speak life into these kids. A few weeks back, he was speaking to a local school's baseball team. Now, he went with the tackle to fish for youth. He went with a message designed to speak to baseball players. But God showed up and did what He does. God used my friend Shannon and his words that day to reach a man who was near seventy years old. This man was a baseball player over fifty years ago. Not only did God show up that day but He also showed out. The man got his life right with God and then a few days later, Shannon baptized him right there on the baseball field in a brand-new water trough. The water trough is where animals come to quench their thirst. The man quenched his eternal thirst that day as well by receiving the living water. The team yelled in excitement as this man showed them what winning looked like. Oh, and that team won the state championship a couple of weeks later.

Then the eleven disciples went to Galilee, to the mountain where Jesus had told them to go. When they saw him, they worshiped him; but some doubted. Then Jesus came to them and said, "All authority in heaven and on earth has been given to me. Therefore go and make disciples of all nations, baptizing them in the name of the Father and of the Son and of the Holy Spirit, and teaching them to obey everything I have commanded you. And surely I am with you always, to the very end of the age." (Matthew 28:16–20 NIV)

We are all going to be a different lure with a different set of skills that will reach different people. Look at my testimony. Whew! I got it all wrong for so long and at fifty, got it right. So many scars, so much hurt, and so much regret, but God still saved me and changed me. My friend Shannon has a completely different testimony. He had some of the same temptations that I did but stayed strong with God where I fell short. I wish I had his testimony in so many ways. My friend Mike has a completely different testimony too. One where divorce and cancer led him to a closer walk with God through surrender and forgiveness. We are just three men out of millions, all of whom have a different testimony. We are just simply different lures in God's tackle box.

In a large house there are articles not only of gold and silver, but also of wood and clay; some are for special purposes and some for common use. Those who cleanse themselves from the latter will be instruments for special purposes, made holy, useful to the Master and prepared to do any good work. (2 Timothy 2:20–21 NIV)

Do not be just a lure for God. Be the *best* lure for God. A lure for a special purpose like the scripture reads.

Questions

1. What has God used to hook you in your life? Have you ever looked at your life through the lens of being a lure for God?
2. Do you think God can use your worst hurt in your life for His glory and His kingdom? Explain.
3. Do you ask God for opportunities to talk about Him? Are you looking for the chance to talk about what Jesus is doing in your life?

Chapter 12

Tell Your Story (The Next Trip)

We all have a story of what our life was like without God and then what it has been like with God. So many people do not tell their testimony because of fear. People say stuff like "Oh, my story is too bad," "If they knew everything I've done, they would kick me out," "God knows my story, and that is personal between Him and me," "My testimony is so bland that it does not have any powerful moments in it," and the excuses go on and on and on.

They triumphed over him by the blood of the Lamb and by the word of their testimony. (Revelation 12:11 NIV)

God's Word says that we defeat the devil by Jesus's blood and the word of our testimony. It is the word with action that you read about earlier in the book. Remember my pastor David's words. We have a job to do, and God has a job to do; let us not get in the way. We must be ready and willing to tell our testimony. We need a one-minute elevator version of what God is doing in our lives. We also need the time to sit down for lunch or coffee to share our full testimony. Telling our testimony is part of our job. It is the only weapon that we have against the devil. We have all kinds of armor, but when we tell how of God's Word came into our lives, it is the sword that we get to use.

I challenge you to write your testimony. Please share it on your social media pages. Tell your good, your bad, and your ugly. Your testimony will matter and make a difference. The devil is going to try to convince you not to write this or that. So I want to encourage you to write them anyway. Tell the whole story. When you let people see all that God has done in your life, it shows just how great our God is. This will be a key part of changing a previous situation from a wound to just a scar. Too many people allow something that they did or something that happened to them to remain a wound their entire lives. Change that wound that is slowly killing you into a scar. A scar is an area that does not hide what happened but leaves a mark that shows that we've recovered from what happened. This is so vital in all our lives. Change your wounds into scars and then let people see your scars.

Just writing this reminds me of when Jacob wrestled with God.

So Jacob was left alone, and a man wrestled with him till daybreak. When the man saw that he could not overpower him, he touched the socket of Jacob's hip so that his hip was wrenched as he wrestled with the man. Then the man said, "Let me go, for it is daybreak." But Jacob replied, "I will not let you go unless you bless me." The man asked him, "What is your name?"

"Jacob," he answered. Then the man said, "Your name will no longer be Jacob, but Israel, because you have struggled with God and with humans and have overcome." Jacob said, "Please tell me your name." But he replied, "Why do you ask my name?" Then he blessed him there. So Jacob called the place Peniel, saying, "It is because I saw God face to face, and yet my life was spared." The sun rose above him as he passed Peniel, and he was limping because of his hip. (Genesis 32:24–31 NIV)

Jacob had a scar from his encounter with God. He was left with a limp. He was also given a new name. Do not miss this. You can *not* have a real encounter with God and be the same as you were before the encounter. You will be different. Remember my own son saying, "I had to come see what changed my dad." I had so many wounds that God made scars. Now, it did not mean that the wounds were not there, and it did not mean that the wounds didn't hurt me or the people around me. It just simply meant that God healed the wounds and left me the reminder that He wants me to use them for His kingdom and glory.

The hurts, pains, and struggles you have had in your life will be used for God's glory. Remember your story but His glory!

Lord God, I pray for the person that is reading this right now. Lord, I pray that their soul belongs to You. I pray that their mind and heart is in better condition than before. I pray, God, that we continue to seek

You and Your will for us. I pray protection over their life as they go about their daily activities. Lord, I pray this person is different because of what You have done in their life. Lord, we are praying for life-changing difference that others will notice and ask about. God, we are thanking You and giving You all the praise and all the glory for everything that you continue to do in our midst. God, thank You for scars. Lord, give us strength, courage, and wisdom to be bold and tell our story for Your glory. I pray for all of this in the name of Jesus. Amen.

Remember that the boat was built to carry many people. Jesus referred to His father's house as big with many rooms. He goes before us to prepare the table for us to dine together. Make sure you do your part to catch as many as possible. There's always room for one more!

Do not let your hearts be troubled. You believe in God; believe also in me. My Father's house has many rooms; if that were not so, would I have told you that I am going there to prepare a place for you? And if I go and prepare a place for you, I will come back and take you to be with me that you also may be where I am. (John 14:1–3 NIV)

Questions

1. Have you ever shared your testimony? If not, what has kept you from sharing it?
2. Does now knowing that your testimony is one of the parts needed to defeat the devil encourage you to begin telling it to others?
3. What can you do to advance the kingdom of God in your family, your work place, and your local church?

Acknowledgments

To Kim, my wife, for the way you prayed when you asked, sought, and even knocked on heaven's door for me. You showed me what the love of God looked like in so many ways. You always saw more in me than I did. You saw me the way God saw me when no one else did. I am forever grateful for your love and your support in everything I have done. Behind every good man is a great woman, and you are the best! I love you!

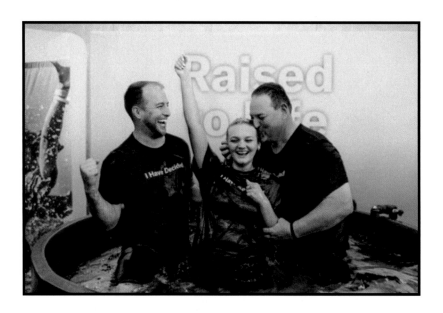

To my friend/pastor David. The way you just allow the Holy Spirit to lead you in how you interact with people is inspirational. Thank you for loving me like you have. You make a difference in so many lives because you go after the one. I am one of those for whom you personally make a difference in my life. I am a better me because of you pouring into my life. We have a job to do, and God has a job to do; let us not get in the way! I love you, man.

To my friend Shannon. The way you love my entire family and speak life into each of us is a blessing in our lives. Brother, it is an honor to do life with you and watch as God uses you to minister to so many people. Thank you for being obedient to the Holy Spirit right when He prompts you. From blessings spoken around small groups to baptisms in a hot tub, I am encouraged by what God does with you. There is always more! I love you, man.

To my friend Mike. The prayers you have prayed over me and with me have been so meaningful to me. You prayed with me when I went all in with God. Your encouragement to get into God's Word and then do our own recap on the ride to work has been life changing to me. The most impactful practice you do, however, is allow me to pray for and pour into your family. We are building a boat! I love you, man.

Printed in the United States
by Baker & Taylor Publisher Services